The Ribbon Stall

Written by Don Long
Illustrated by Spike Wademan

Characters

Ishrat   Jimnah

Sanjukta   Bob

Customers   Mr Little (Bob's dad)

Mr Little: Here we are kids, at the world-**renowned** Portobello Road Street Market.

Sanjukta: We've still got an hour to set up our **stall**. I hope this idea works.

Jimnah: It's got to. How else are we going to raise the money?

Mr Little: It's a good idea, Jimnah. As far as I know, no one else has ever thought of it… and I've had a stall here since my old dad died. And he had a stall before that.

Sanjukta: Well, thank you for helping us pay the insurance, Mr Little…

Bob: …and to **register**…

Jimnah: …and pay for today.

Mr Little: That's okay. But you've still got the hard work ahead of you.

Ishrat: Will you check on us from time to time?

Mr Little: Of course! I'll be just around the corner at my fruit stall. Remember, the market starts at eight. Good luck.

Bob: Hey Jimnah, what did you guys write on our stall sign? I understand "The Ribbon Stall" in English, but…

Jimnah: Oh, it just says "The Ribbon Stall" in **Urdu**, **Bengali**, and **Swahili**, too.

Ishrat: Hey, let's put out some more bookmarks.

Jimnah: Remember Ishrat, Bob's dad said not to put out too much of our **stock** at first.

Bob: Jimnah's right. I've helped my dad on his stall lots of times. The trick is to just put out a few things, sell those, and keep replacing them from the stock.

Sanjukta: Okay, but let's put up a few more kite tails. They look really good, and these Himalayan prayer ribbons should sell okay.

Jimnah: Look out Sanjukta, here comes a customer.

Customer: A ribbon stall. I've never heard of one of these before.

Ishrat: We're new.

Jimnah: It's a fresh idea.

Bob: There are thousands of things you can do with ribbons.

Customer: These look interesting, what are they?

Sanjukta: They're kite ribbons.

Customer: They look really great. And they'd pack easily into my suitcase. But I don't have a kite.

Ishrat: You don't need one. They look great flying from a balcony…

Jimnah: …or hanging in a flat…

Bob: …or wrapped around a present.

Sanjukta: In fact, they make great presents themselves.

Customer: You've convinced me. And that's a great price. I'll take one. It'll make a great present for my niece.

Bob: Ishrat, how are we doing on overall sales?

Ishrat: We're not doing too badly, Bob, but raising enough money for our **contribution** to the school trip to Normandy still seems a long way off.

Sanjukta: Look Bob, here comes your dad.

Mr Little: How's it going, **colleagues**? Did you have enough change in your **float**?

Bob: The float's fine, Dad. We haven't run out of change. But sales are **sluggish**.

Jimnah: Yeah, that lady over there selling candles is doing way better than us.

Sanjukta: It's not like we aren't selling anything. It's just that we aren't selling enough.

Mr Little: I think I see the problem. You've got to let the **punters** think they're getting a bargain. Why don't you try selling some of your stuff by the metre with discounts if they buy a lot? See how that goes. Look, here comes another customer. Quick, change your sign.

Customer: So, how does the discount work?

Ishrat: The more centimetres you buy, the cheaper it gets.

Customer: So if I buy a metre it's cheaper than half a metre.

Jimnah: Yes, and if you buy 1.5 metres the price drops by a third again.

Sanjukta: And for 1.75 metres the price per metre drops even more.

Customer: That's a great deal. I'll take… hmm… let me see… why don't you give me 2.75 metres of this one? Show me how long that would be…

Bob: No problem!

Customer: Great, I think I'll take another 1.5 metres. My friend might like to use this type of ribbon for her crafts.

Ishrat: Wow, sales are booming now. Hey Jimnah, let's take the first lunch break and visit Bob's dad at his fruit stall.

Mr Little: Get your fruit here! Melons, berries! Oh, hello you two, ready for some lunch? How's it going?

Ishrat: Really good. But my head's starting to spin with decimal numbers and discounts and fractions.

Jimnah: Like, how much more should 200 millimetres of ribbon be compared to two metres?

Mr Little: So it's working then. Good. Now, take some of these plums over there to Mrs Colvin and she'll give you some bagels. And Ishrat, you take some of this marmalade to Mikey in that shop and exchange it for some of his home-made fudge.

Jimnah: But Mr Little…

Mr Little: Go on. Don't be shy. We stall holders look after one another. What goes around comes around.

Bob: Hey, Sanjukta, there's only an hour to go. I've got an idea. Where's the marker pen? Jimnah, how do you spell "**remnants**" in Swahili? And we should write it in Urdu and Bengali, too.

Sanjukta: Here, you'd better let me and Ishrat do it. You'll never get the **characters** right!

Customer: What are you writing?

Bob: "Remnants." There's only an hour to go until the market closes at 6:30. It's only the remnants left. So we're dropping our prices.

Customer:	So, what are these?
Sanjukta:	They were kite tails.
Bob:	And these were prayer flags.
Ishrat:	But now they're remnants.
Jimnah:	The more centimetres you buy, the cheaper they get per centimetre.
Customer:	What about this one, then. It's pretty.
Bob:	Let me measure it. It's 55.75 centimetres.
Customer:	That would look nice in my daughter's hair. I'll take it. How much is it?
Sanjukta:	I'll just figure the price out for you on the calculator.

Ishrat: Phew! What a day. It's gone past 6:30.

Mr Little: So, how did it go?

Jimnah: Better than we expected!

Ishrat: It won't take much longer at all for us each to have enough for the school trip.

Sanjukta: Yeah, like you with Bob, our parents said that if we could earn half…

Bob: …you'd pay for the rest!

Mr Little: And so we will! Though don't forget you've got to subtract the float.

Bob, Jimnah, Ishrat, and Sanjukta: We already have!